Marriage and Equality

How Natural Marriage Upholds Equality for Children

By Jennifer Johnson

Foreword by Leila Miller

Published by the Ruth Institute

*We are creating a Christ-like mass social movement
to end the agony and injustice of family breakdown.*

Published by:
The Ruth Institute
4845 Lake Street, Suite 217
Lake Charles, LA 70605
info@ruthinstitute.org

Ordering information:
Discounts are available on quantity purchases. Contact the publisher at above address for details.

Marriage and Equality/Jennifer Johnson—3rd Edition
ISBN: 978-0-692-94099-0

Dedication

This book is dedicated to my whole family, especially my children, their families, and all my posterity.

I also dedicate it to everyone raised in a "diverse family structure," who intuits that something isn't right with it. Maybe this book will help them articulate what they feel.

Immaculate Heart of Mary, pray for us.

Table of Contents

Foreword

When I picked up Jennifer Johnson's *Marriage and Equality* (first edition) several months ago, I was intrigued by the idea of "equality" as a way to ensure a child's natural right to an intact family. Equality is not a traditional virtue, but it is the predominant value of our culture today, a concept destined to catch the attention of a modern reader. I read the book straight through in one sitting, and I knew after the first few pages that this short, clear, and completely original work would become a valuable and standard resource for all those who care about the effects of divorce, and other forms of so-called "diverse" family structures, on children. Since that day, this powerful little book has never been far from my mind.

They say a picture paints a thousand words, and throughout *Marriage and Equality*, Jennifer Johnson employs simple but brilliant diagrams to drive home, visually, the familial burdens carried by children who were raised in "diverse" family structures. Though the children's sufferings have their origin in their genetic parents' rejection of each other, these sufferings do not subsequently fade away; in fact, the children continue to shoulder these burdens for decades, burdens that often become more complicated, layered, and heavy--even transferred to the next generation.

As a now-adult child of divorce, Johnson did not fully understand the pervasive pain she felt from her own family break-up until, upon an inspiration, she began to draw her family structure on paper. She walks us through her own surprise as she saw the striking and disturbing results of her drawings. Far from the simple symmetry of an intact family structure, the diagrams of her broken family were spider-like, even frightening. Other simple diagrams convey, in one glance, how a child in certain "diverse" family forms must compartmentalize and segment his life when moving back and forth between two (or more) families and their unique dynamics.

As it will for readers of the book, the marked inequality between intact and "diverse" families jumped out at Johnson. With sudden clarity, she understood the inherent and simple unfairness of "diverse" families for a child, as it sets up that child for hardships and handicaps that simply do not exist for children of intact families like me.

I am now keenly and permanently cognizant of a hidden pain and injustice that I had not noticed before. For nearly five decades, I went about my life completely unaware that all around me, every day, people carry unwanted burdens and consequences from their parents' rejection of each other, while I walk through my life relatively unencumbered. The realization of that inequality and injustice continues to impact me to this day.

This dramatic service to the reader--the shock of having one's eyes opened so simply and powerfully--is the genius of *Marriage and Equality*. The child of a "diverse" family structure may finally understand why "this never feels right," and the rest of us will respond with attention and compassion to the inequality we never saw before. Together, all of us will be motivated to end the scourge of ubiquitous divorce, out of wedlock childbearing, third-part reproduction, and other "diverse" family forms, which are the cause of so much individual pain, generational chaos, and dysfunction in our society.

Leila Miller, editor of *Primal Loss: The Now-Adult Children of Divorce Speak*
August 2017

Introduction

You are reading a book that may help you understand family breakdown in a new way. It is like a journey through unexplored territory. Equality is the main tool that we will use to navigate this journey. Think of equality like a measuring rod. It will help us understand the problems created by family breakdown and so-called "family diversity," not from the outside as somebody perusing social science data, but from the inside, as somebody who lived it.

I believe that I am the first person to use equality as a way to map this journey. Because of this, I needed to create new phrases to express what I saw, such as "structural equality," "horizontal equality," "vertical equality," and "pregnancy-free coitus." I introduce these with some trepidation because even though I considered each of these phrases very carefully, I worry that they might create difficulties for readers. Even so, I had to name what I saw. If in the future I think of better ways to name what I saw, or if I receive suggestions, I may change them.

My intended audience is comprised of:

- Parents (married, unmarried, or remarried)
- Anybody interested in family policy
- Anybody who believes that equality is an important ideal

- Anybody raised outside the marriage of their own genetic mother and father

This argument is based on the story of my life and everything I have learned in recent years about what the Catholic Church teaches about sex and marriage, which is what all Christians believed about those things until just a few decades ago. I had a highly chaotic childhood, and because of that, you may feel my emotions about it from time to time as you read these pages.

If you were raised with your own married mother and father, it may be tempting to view the adults in my situation as idiosyncratic and unusual. But as I hope to show, the issues I present here don't have a lot to do with character. I have deliberately excluded interpersonal family dynamics from the argument, because I am trying to avoid something called the "fundamental attribution error." This error is when we evaluate somebody's behavior based on what we believe is their internal disposition or their character. To avoid the error, we need to include the context of that behavior, which includes situational and cultural pressures. Our culture exerts certain influences regarding sex that must be considered. Plus, the family structure itself influences the adults, whatever form it has. It imposes its own rules quite apart from the character of the adults who occupy it. Please do not infer anything about the character of the adults in my life as you read this; try to look at family structure as its own reality apart from how parents behave on a day-to-day basis.

Readers also need to know that my parents had a "good divorce." They split up when I was three, and they did not argue, they were civil with each other, my dad paid his child support payments promptly for the most part, they almost never spoke badly about the other in front of me, and they shared me on holidays. They managed their relationship with each other and the logistical details of my day-to-day life the way the experts advised.

There is a time and place for people like me to give our testimony and use our life stories to make an argument for a certain position. But I can only run so far with the equality argument I present here. If you like what you read here, I ask that you consider how to make it in your own way, with your own observations of your life or the lives of people around you who were not raised inside the lifelong marriage of their own mother and father. This is especially true for those of you who have no experience of family structure inequality. In some respects, your voice may be more important than mine. At the very least, don't discount the value of your voice. People may respect you more, since you have some objectivity that I may lack.

Regarding the phrase "natural marriage." I define this as life-long marriage between one man and one woman who are open to procreating their own children through their lovemaking. I do not take into account the religious or baptismal status of the spouses when making this argument. Since I am Catholic, it is not my intention to present an argument that is contrary to Catholic teaching. It is only my intention to focus on family structure from the child's point of view. I offer information so that adults can make more-informed long-term decisions.

A note about the word "triangle." I utilize the geometric shape of the triangle to represent the intact family founded on natural marriage. Some people refer to this as the biological family, but for my purposes here, I prefer to think of it as the ontological family. Ontology is a word from philosophy meaning, "the branch of metaphysics dealing with the nature of being." The intact family of married father and mother is the family structure that best reflects a child's being, his physical origins, back to the child. Like a mirror that reflects our image back to us, our married mother and father are each half of how our bodies came into being. My argument is that their one-flesh union serves as a mirror for us regarding the origin of our bodies, who we look like, where we obtained certain traits, etc.

I do not claim that what I present here is the definitive defense of marriage. I only hope to show how natural marriage provides a better defense of equality for children than any of the alternatives for marriage and childbearing. Children grow into adults, so this kind of equality stays with them for their whole lives. Since equality is a primary ideal in our culture, it seems only fair to apply it to children's family structures, especially since the social science data clearly delineates between kids raised with their own married mother and father, and those not raised in that way.

Finally, I hope this argument will make the defense of natural marriage more accessible to Democrats, liberals, the younger generation, and pro-life advocates who don't defend natural marriage.

What this book is not

This is not a philosophical treatise on why marriage is only between one man and one woman. Others have defended that idea from a philosophical perspective much better than I do here. This is a practical book, not a philosophical one.

This is not a child rearing book. I am not giving parents advice on day-to-day matters regarding their children.

This is not scholarly research. This is the story of how I was raised without my own married mother and father, what I came to believe about marriage because of that experience, and how I was able to apply what I experienced to other forms of so-called "family diversity."

This is not a brand-new revelation. Have you ever played Rummy Tiles? Have you ever needed to rearrange the entire board so that you could play one of your tiles? That is a good analogy for what I have done here. I have taken many important ideas that were already widely known and rearranged them so that I could insert my life story into them and have it—finally—make sense to me.

Christian social conservatives believe in equality but may not realize it

This is an image of the Holy Family that I used to keep in my office.

I would look at this image from time to time and pray to Jesus for wisdom for defending marriage and the family.

One day I was looking at this image and saw a triangle between the head of Jesus, His mother Mary, her husband Joseph, then back to Jesus. I thought to myself, "Wow, that's the family structure! It's a triangle! It is not only a reflection of the Holy Family, it is a reflection of the Trinity!"

This excited me for a couple reasons. For one thing, I've discovered that the average person doesn't understand what "family structure" or "structural issues" mean. Policy wonks, like me, tend to take for granted that others understand us when we use those phrases. To be able to show the family as a triangle means that the average person now has a simple way to understand what those phrases mean.

I was also excited because I wondered how it would apply to my own childhood. I had not been raised with my own married parents. My parents divorced when I was three and went on to subsequent marriages, divorces, different children, a lot of back and forth between "two homes," and a lot of chaos.

I went home that night and applied the family triangle to my situation. I carefully drew it all out, using several pieces of paper. It took me several tries to get everybody to fit onto the page in a way that made sense and was proportional. As I worked on it, I could tell that it was going to be far more complex than I had *ever* imagined. This is what I saw:

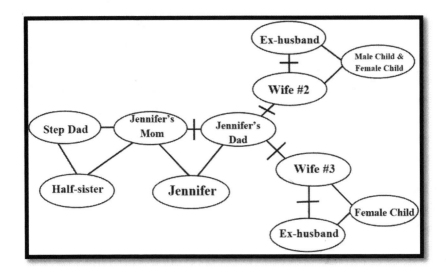

That's me, in the bottom center circle. What do you think? What is your gut response to this? The first few hours after I finished the drawing were surreal, and I was in a daze. Seriously, what is this? How was I supposed to navigate this *as a child, alone*?

In fact, I didn't navigate it at all. I blocked parts out as time went on, out of necessity. My kids will confirm that I never talked about my childhood while they were growing up. For one thing, I had no intellectual framework through which to understand it. All I knew was that it was chaotic and painful, and that I felt ashamed about it.

It was such a shock to see it all there in a two-dimensional way. I had a flood of emotions come over me, as it brought back memories of people that left my life due to divorce, so I was supposed to have forgotten them when that happened.

One of the first things that stuck out at me was how ugly it is. It looked like a malformed spider's web. It was not pretty like the simple triangle I had seen. My initial excitement turned to tears of sadness. And so I cried, a lot at first.

As time went on, I became angry at God for showing this to me. I couldn't understand why He would make me feel old pain like that. Why bring it all up again? Why have this ugly family structure burned into my mind now? Wasn't I better off just burying it all in the back of my mind, as if it never happened? The diagram reminded me of my shame. It was always very difficult to have so many different adults to reckon with constantly, and I didn't like having them thrust into my face again all at once. Is it safe for me to say that I just wanted my own family? MY family, MY triad, MY home?

Christian social conservatives believe in equality for children, because they believe in this for every child:

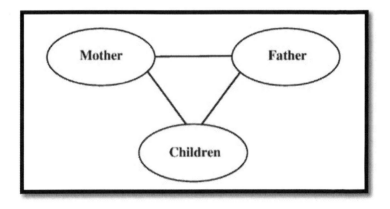

Embracing the liberal value of equality may strengthen our position

I work at the Ruth Institute with Dr. Jennifer Roback Morse. I first saw this form of equality one day when talking to Dr. Morse about her childhood. I asked her, "How many kids had divorced parents when you were young?" She said that she could think of one.

In my mind, I pictured the playground, with her and her schoolmates on it. I imagined each of them with a diagram of their family structure above their heads in a little bubble like a cartoon. All the kids had the intact triangle, except for one (shown in the lower left corner in the image above).

It was a way that they were all the same, except for one student. When I saw this image in my mind, I knew then that this was an equality issue for us. But conservatives are not known for valuing equality as a primary ideal. If they do address equality regarding the marriage issue, they might say that it is OK to treat different types of couples differently, that it is OK to deny marriage rights to same-sex couples, since from a reproductive standpoint they are different from opposite-sex couples.

It is a logical rebuttal and I agree with it, but it doesn't demonstrate a commitment to equality. So many opposite-sex couples contracept and abort, and we don't deny them civil marriage licenses. I know that they are not in charge of their fertility to the degree that they imagine, but I've talked to enough people to know that they really do believe they have 100% control over their fertility, like a spigot. It also seems that many fertile opposite-sex couples believe that they have some sort of right or entitlement for pregnancy-free coitus.

Let's assume for a moment that those ideas are true, that people really do have 100% control over their fertility and that fertile couples have a right or entitlement for pregnancy-free coitus. Given that mentality, isn't it much easier to understand the argument for same-sex marriage? Shedding light on this mentality in this way may explain why its supporters believe that Christian social conservatives aren't arguing in good faith. Same-sex marriage supporters may believe that Christian social conservatives think as they do regarding the right to pregnancy-free coitus.

There has been some head-scratching among conservatives about why our arguments for marriage did not carry the day. I think the main problem is that the Sexual Revolution is like a flood. So much social "landscape" has already been destroyed by it, and the flood just keeps rising. For example, after the Windsor decision in 2013, which struck down the Defense of Marriage Act, I had every expectation two years later that the United States Supreme Court would legalize same-sex marriage throughout the United States. The flood waters would continue to rise, and this was painfully obvious to me. Whatever little levees and barricades we erected would continue be swept away in the flood. We had not stopped it at any other juncture, and so I knew we wouldn't be able to stop it at the same-sex marriage juncture.

But I wonder: what if the pro-marriage movement had appealed to people's sense of justice and fairness? Let's look at the pro-life movement, for example. On February 21, 2017, Crux published remarks by Daniel K. Williams, author of *Defenders of the Unborn*, a book about the history of the pro-life movement. He makes the observation that the pro-life movement started as a liberal movement based on social justice and human rights. He believes that the movement gains vitality and appeal when its proponents frame the issue using liberal values.

I discovered that we can do the same thing by embracing the liberal value of equality. The ancient Christian teaching on sex and marriage means that every child is to be raised with his or her own married mother and father, except for an unavoidable tragedy. That's a type of equality that people don't talk about, but it is real. And there are other equalities that flow out of that one. When the family breaks down or doesn't form according to the triad, I will show how the inequalities for children multiply. I think it is exciting to see that this form of equality has been the flipside of the ancient Christian teaching on marriage and sex all along.

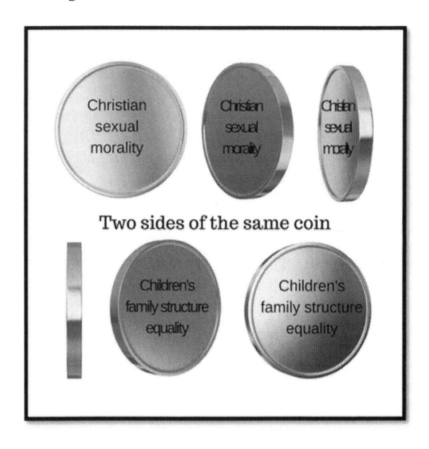

Two sides of the same coin

I am not suggesting that we abandon our other arguments, and it is clear to me that this argument does not supplant them. My hope is that it will make them palatable to an audience that puts equality above any other ideal.

The many ways that natural marriage creates structural equality, and eliminates structural inequalities, for children

I have observed several ways that natural marriage creates equality for children.

First way: horizontal equality

When the ancient Christian teachings on sex and marriage are followed on a wide scale, every child lives with his own married mother and father in a unified home, except for an unavoidable tragedy. Family dynamics are structurally equal between full-blooded siblings. When Christian sexual ethics are practiced, most children will have the intact triad founded on natural marriage.

Christian sexual ethics creates "structural" equality among children—they're all with their own parents. None of them are shuttling back and forth between "two homes." None of them have had a genetic parent/family severed from them due to being conceived as a result of anonymous sperm or egg donation. None of them have birth records that have been falsified to accommodate a non-genetic parent's wishes.

Remember the image with the kids on the playground? A school playground today will have children with all kinds of family structures, with only about 40% having the intact triangle. The horizontal form of equality I describe here has dropped dramatically in recent decades, and I believe it corresponds directly with the Sexual Revolution.

This drop in structural equality among children has a fancy name among the Sexual Revolutionaries. They call it, "family structure diversity." It seems to be a way to affirm the adults who make those "choices." But the social science data is clear about the negative outcomes for children not raised with their married parents, so I call it "family structure inequality."

Related to this is the complicated family structure that gets created by divorces and remarriages. Here is an example of the complicated layers that can develop for children who are born into a first marriage, whose parents divorce and remarry. When parents stay together, this doesn't happen.

Step-families are complicated

Step-families have various layers of complicated relationships & rules. Layers often build on each other. Rules that apply to children in one layer may not apply to children in another layer. There can be more or less than five layers.

Layer 5: one or both parents divorces again.

Layer 4: one or both parents has a child with step-parent.

Layer 3: step-parent(s) may have step children from a prior relationship.

Layer 2: mother and/or father remarry. Each spends more time with new spouse than with child.

Layer 1: mother and father divorce. Child now lives in 2 homes.

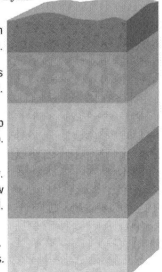

There is no equality between the children in these layers, but aren't parents supposed to at least try to treat their children equally?

Second way: vertical equality

Family structure equality means that the acceptance of *all* family members is a two-way street between parents and their children. Natural marriage upholds equality by creating equality between parents and their children, between the older generation and the younger generation. Let me use an anecdote from my own life to illustrate what I mean.

When I was growing up, I spent my entire childhood doing the back-and-forth thing between "two homes." My parents both remarried so I had two half-time dads. I was about twelve or so when I consciously understood that my two half-time dads did not equal one dad. To a casual observer, it might seem as though me being with each of them for half-time would be the same as having one whole dad. But it was not. I am not totally sure how I came to this realization, but I do remember consciously thinking it as I stood in the driveway one day. I also remember feeling terrible about the messed-up nature of my family, how alone I was in it, and how it was never going to change. I am pretty sure this realization happened before my dad married for the third time.

Perhaps I came to this realization because I was an eye-witness to what an intact family and a full-time dad looked like. My step-dad was a full-time dad to my half-sister. She lived with both her married parents, my mom and my step-dad. I could see that what she had and what I had were two different things. The divorce and remarriages placed a double standard upon me, an unreciprocated requirement. I was treated differently from the adults around me in a very specific way, related to how my family was structured.

In each home, I was required to pretend that my other parent (and that parents' family) did not exist. So while in my mother's home, I had to pretend that my father and his family did not exist, and while in my father's home, I had to pretend that my mother and her family did not exist.

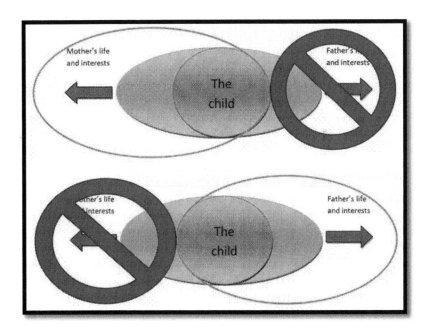

For example, family photos of other people's whole families were on the walls, but not of my whole family. Group family photos were taken and hung on the walls, but since I wasn't a full-fledged daughter of the new families my parents created, I wasn't in those photos. I know this is not unique to me as I've read other anecdotes by step-children telling the same kind of story.

I was the only one who had divided Christmases, divided holidays, and divided birthdays. I've seen this referred to as "two Christmases," or "two birthdays" in some divorce literature as a way to sugar-coat the vertical inequality. My dad wasn't welcome on Christmas morning, and my mom wasn't welcome on Christmas Eve. I don't think either of them would have come, had they been invited. They were too busy with their new families. And when I got a little older and my parents lived further apart, I traveled alone during the holidays to see each of them. None of the adults in my life had to do any of those things. It was a requirement placed upon me that made their lives easier.

Our "no-fault" divorce mentality means that the child receives this message from one or both parents: "I am willing to spend half of your childhood apart from you. I do not want to live with you full time anymore, and there is no adult in your life who does. Living with you full time is too hard. It means that I must live with your other parent, and I am 'choosing' not to do that. Even though your other parent did not commit any grave fault, I am willing to miss half your childhood."

If the other parent committed a grave fault, then the child should not be going there very much, and certainly should not be living there. But since the child is going there and possibly living there, then the child is being put into a scandalous situation and has nobody there to help him navigate it. The child receives an implicit message that the parent isn't that bad. But either the parent is a threat or he (or she) is not. That is an objective fact. If he is a threat to such an extent that a divorce is warranted, then why is the child going there? If he is not a threat to such an extent, then the divorce should not have occurred. If that parent is good enough for the child, then he (or she) is good enough for the other parent. Our false idea of "liberty" creates a fake foundation for the child's life post-divorce.

It really never ends, and I have a recent example of it still playing out. In about 2014 my dad's sister met my step-dad's brother for the first time. Quite innocently, he remarked, "I didn't know Jim (my dad) had a sister." Of course. How would he know? My dad had three sisters, but I never talked about them. I know he meant it innocently, and he has always been very kind to me. But it is a good example of the dynamic I'm describing. I did not have one person who was a full time, 24/7 parent. Nobody wanted to be with me on a full-time basis... at least, that was how it felt. How is this justice? How is this family?

To use an analogy from the business world, it was as if I was the side-job for one parent, then the side-job for the other, back and forth, back and forth, back and forth like this. I was not the full-time "job" for either of my parents. I had no sense of permanent family, yet my parents went on to create new full-time families for themselves. It was very much like living in a hall of mirrors and the double standards were like a thorn in my mind that I could not understand or remove. For these and other reasons, I now believe that making a child live in two homes is contrary to divine law (a concept that Protestant and Evangelical Christians might call "Biblical principles").

The "two homes" arrangement has the endorsement of many experts and leaders, people who are smarter than I am and who are better educated than I am. Yet they have not figured out that these kids have no single person who is with them as a parent on a full-time basis. Or, they have figured it out and they don't see a problem with it.

I know there will be some who are tempted to think that my experience is unique to me, but it is not. It is the dynamic of what happens when genetic parents reject each other, and when experts and leaders endorse this rejection. Let's look at other types of non-triad arrangements to see what I mean.

Think about the kids who are conceived from anonymous sperm or anonymous eggs. They have to pretend that half of who they are does not exist. It is unlikely that their parents have to do the same. Here is the same diagram as above, cropped to show what it looks like in a household of a single-dad-by-choice, or a gay (male) household.

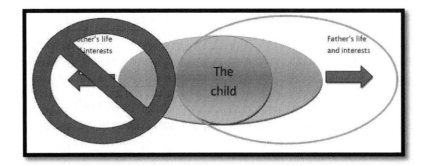

The reverse is true in a single-mom-by-choice household, or a lesbian household.

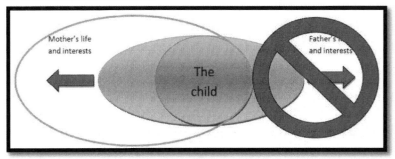

A study was conducted in 2010 of young adults who had been conceived through sperm donation. Two-thirds of them agreed with this statement: "My sperm donor is half of who I am." You can see the similarity between what those kids go through, and what the kids of divorce go through.

We are still talking about the vertical form of equality created by natural marriage, so let's consider the parents in these situations. If the parents were raised inside the intact triad, then there is an inequality between the parents and the children. There are two different standards being applied. The child must pretend that half of himself does not exist, while the child's parents don't have to do the same. The child acknowledges those parents, the grandparents, their aunts and uncles, etc. But one-half of that child's genetic family has been discarded and is not acknowledged by the parents. The parent, as a child, was raised around people who resemble him (or her). But, depending on the circumstances, the child has only half of his family that he resembles (the genetic parent's family), and half that he does not resemble (the social parent's family). Again, in this respect, it is similar to what I experienced, since once my parents remarried, I acquired social (aka, step) parents.

When family acceptance is a two-way street, that is vertical equality. The parents are treating the kids the same way that the kids treat the parents. Everybody's full families are acknowledged. When family acceptance is a one-way street, that is vertical inequality, inequality between the generations. The older generation gets preferential treatment. The younger generation must accept whatever the adults "choose" to give. Children are observant. Any school-aged child can see which of them live with their own married parents and which do not. They can see that some kids know and are connected to both halves of their origins, and others are not. If a particular child thinks or feels something about the inequality in which he finds himself, his thoughts and feelings may not be welcome. This is because they *cannot* be welcome. To welcome those thoughts and feelings might cast doubt upon the structure of the family itself. For example, if a child conceived with anonymous sperm later wants to know where his dad is, will those thoughts and feelings be welcomed by his caretakers? Often times, the answer seems to be, "No." As for myself, I would have been terrified to reveal that I wanted to live with both of my parents. I was never asked directly, but if I had been, I am sure I would have lied about it.

I wonder if these environments fit the psychological description of "invalidating environments." According to David M. Allen, M.D., in his article, "Invalidation in Families: What Are The Hidden Aspects?" from *Psychology Today,* an invalidating environment is one where "the opinions of the target are invalid, irrational, selfish, uncaring, stupid, most likely insane, and wrong, wrong, wrong."

Third way: permitted grief versus disenfranchised grief

Not only does the inequality happen on the level of the family, it happens in the wider culture. The child lives under a burden and is not allowed to feel anything negative about the particular family form that was chosen for him. If he feels grief about missing half of himself, it is "disenfranchised grief," grief that is not acceptable to the wider culture. Why might this be?

The Sexual Revolution was a cultural revolution that changed the cultural presumptions surrounding sex, marriage and childbearing. It seems to have created a culture of sex with its own taboos, initiation rites, rites of passage, and ideas of pollution and purification. Our culture is profoundly concerned about adults and their happiness in their sexual, marital and reproductive "choices." Much like a factory that earns more profit when it does not have to account for the pollution it generates, the negative consequences of "sexual liberation" are pushed on to subsequent generations who are then subjected to its inequalities and are denied their grief.

As a culture, we failed to understand that by loosening those old restrictions, the old consequences and taboos did not simply evaporate and disappear. They only shifted to another realm. For example, I think it is fair to say that there is a taboo in regards to talking about how harmful certain family structures are.

Put more simply: adults' happiness with their family structure choices *as adults* is more important than their happiness *as children* regarding those same things. All of this is going on, even in the face of all the social science data saying that kids fare best with their own married father and mother.

I know somebody will say, "What about all of the gay parenting studies that show 'no difference'?" They are methodologically flawed, for one thing. For example, one of the most popular and most cited studies used tiny sample sizes and convenience samples, which are a sample of people who are easy for the researcher to reach. The problem with using that kind of sample is that the results cannot be taken to represent the entire population.

For another thing, think about it from this angle: how do gay parents get kids? They do so by some way that has already been shown to increase risk factors for children, such as divorce, adoption and third-party reproduction. When you boil it down, gay parenting advocates are essentially arguing that gay parenting is not equal to the intact triad founded on natural marriage, *it is superior*, since the logic of their argument means that they overcome all the risk factors that are associated with the only methods they can use to obtain children.

Furthermore, the same thing happened when divorce laws were being liberalized starting in the early 1970s, which shot up the divorce rate. The professionals all said the kids would be fine if the adults were happy, that kids are resilient, and that babies are blank slates. That turned out to be false, but the mental health profession has not repudiated its error and those euphemisms have not died out. Not many people realize that "Kids are resilient" relies on an unspoken premise: "Adults are fragile, so we must tiptoe around their sexual, marital, and reproductive choices. We don't want to offend them."

It is a strange sort of "win-win" for people to be raised with their own married mother and father, then grow up to champion unequal family structures for the next generation, including for their own children. I say it is a "win-win," since they get two benefits. First, they received the ongoing benefits of being raised in the intact triad founded on natural marriage. Second, as adults they get to appear open-minded and tolerant of others' sexual and reproductive choices. All the while, they never had to live as a child under what they advocate. For those of us who did, our grief about these injustices is not acknowledged, since the injustice itself must remain unacknowledged. As long as it remains unacknowledged by the wider culture, adults can continue to experience those "freedoms" without guilt.

Part of the healing process is having the freedom to talk about it without being judged or pathologized, free to develop language and concepts to understand it better, and free to advocate for policies that will prevent it from happening to others in the future. That is a kind of equality that we are now denied in the popular culture. While it is true that we can go to therapy for our issues, my own therapy sessions and the two psychology courses I took at the undergraduate level did not teach me *anything* about what I described here and how the Sexual Revolution created and sustains it. All the diagrams were my own idea (except the very first one, the intact triangle, which was inspired). I didn't learn from the mental health profession that the reason I joined a cult as a young adult was that I was trying to escape the chaos that entered my life when my parents divorced, then later remarried. I ceased to exist as a full-fledged daughter in my own family, because my family ceased to exist. It threw me into an "in-between" state. It was and is not only painful, but confusing, contradictory, and exhausting.

I am not criticizing any individual therapist. I know for a fact that many of them, as individuals, mean well. However, I *am* criticizing the mental health industry. I guarantee that my parents had no idea of the dynamics they were putting into motion when they split up. How would they?

When it comes to the structure of the family, the overarching concern in the mental health community seems to be about supporting adults in whatever they decide to do in regard to children's family structures. Our ontology is disregarded, and our family structures are viewed like Gumby play-toys that can be molded and twisted into whatever configuration suits the adults. Plus, the entertainment industry, the business industry, and the legal community are all fully supportive of that framework. This means that they all are entrenching the disregard for natural marriage, the family founded upon it, and the kind of equality it creates for children.

Confronting hypocrisy

You wouldn't believe the profane things total strangers have said to me about my advocacy for natural marriage. Sometimes I ask them, "Were you raised by your own married parents?" and either they don't answer, or the answer is, "Yes." Given what the social science data says regarding outcomes, it is upsetting when these people take their intact families for granted. I'm sure you know people like this. They were raised by their own married parents, yet they are opposed to divorce reform, they advocate for same-sex marriage and same-sex parenting, and they advocate for third-party reproduction (sperm/egg donation; surrogacy).

For example, there is a popular LGBT activist named Masha Gessen, who is also known for writing a biography of Vladimir Putin. In 2014, she was praised by John Kerry at a State Department function for LGBT foreign affairs. In 2012 she made a public statement about how she thinks marriage should be abolished so children can have a subjective number of legal parents. She is one of the few people who understands the connection between marriage and parentage, and she explicitly mentioned this link.

Evidently, between the different ex-lovers and their children, there are three children between five adults. She wants all five of those parents' names to be listed on the kids' birth records.

Think about how a birth certificate is structured. There is a section for the father and the mother, and we can think of this like a mirror of the marriage certificate, with its section for the husband and the wife. This "mirror" analogy explains why birth certificates must be altered to accommodate same-sex marriage.

When I came across Gessen's remarks, something dawned on me. Thanks to the family structure diagram that I made in late 2013, I realized that *I had five parents*: a mom and two step-moms, a dad and one step-dad. Because of the divorces, and the need to ignore half of my family no matter where I was, I had not put it all together that way until I created the diagram. And even then, it wasn't until I encountered Gessen's remarks that I mentally numbered the parental figures from my childhood.

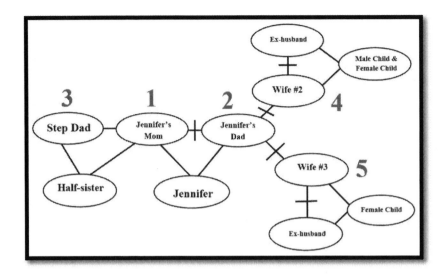

Then I did a little internet-sleuthing, and discovered that she was raised in the intact triad founded on natural marriage. So, she literally has NO IDEA what it is like to live *as a child* under what she's advocating. But I do. There is no way I want all those people to be my legal parents. That's crazy, full stop. But let's look at a practical consideration of her proposal. Instead of going back and forth between "two homes," I would have had three homes or even more. I say this because there is no legal or cultural pressure for adults to create a singular, stable and unified home for their children. Doing that to a child, so that the adults can have a revolving door of semi-permanent sex partners, makes my blood boil.

Listening to those who have lived it

It's important to take into account those who have actually lived through these cultural and legal changes as children. Be sure to listen very carefully to what they say. For example, in 2011 the state of Iowa was proposing to put an amendment into the constitution upholding marriage as between one man and one woman. Hearings were held at the capitol. Among those giving testimony was a young man named Zach Wahls. He was conceived with anonymous sperm, and raised by his lesbian mother and her lover. He gave testimony on their behalf, against the proposed amendment, and a video of his testimony went viral.

When I first saw the video, I knew immediately why people want him to speak for them. I have also read his book, called *My Two Moms: Lessons of Love, Strength, and What Makes a Family*. It is clear to me that Zach is intelligent, articulate, and a sensitive soul. He was born the year my eldest daughter was born, and as I read it, the fondness for him that I felt while watching his video grew. He strikes me as somebody who is sincere and really does want to do the right thing.

He said something during the video that stood out to me. Referring to his sister, he said: "We actually have the same anonymous donor, so we're full siblings, which is really cool for me." I'm glad that he has this sister, but I must also point out the wider perspective. If the dad does not matter, as we must accept under the umbrella of "lesbian marriage and parenting," then why did Zach care that his sister is full blooded? If dads don't matter, then any man's sperm could have been used for his sister, right?

While reading his book, I saw that I am not the first person to notice this remark about his sister. Much of the book was a defense of LGBT marriage rights, and a refutation of conservative arguments regarding LGBT parents being incapable of raising well-adjusted and competent citizens. It is clear that his mother loves him very much and he seems to have had a good and relatively normal upbringing. However, in his book, he did not explain why it was cool for his sister to be full-blooded, he did not address how he feels about possibly having an unknown number of half-siblings from the sperm donor, and he did not address the conservative objection to children witnessing public nudity and sexual activity at LGBT Pride parades.

Until recently I would have said that my own experience as a child in a "diverse" family structure was fine, even though deep down I knew that something was terribly wrong. There is no incentive for kids like us to explore deeper feelings we might have about how our family is structured, and every incentive to ignore or hide any negative feelings we have about it. Because of false ideas like, "Kids are resilient," and, "Babies are blank slates," our parents built their lives atop our ontological loss. They may have done it with good intentions, but the loss remains. I see a role-reversal in these situations, where the child must sacrifice his feelings so that the parent does not have to feel uncomfortable about way the family is structured.

Here is what Zach's family looks like when we apply the family triangle to it:

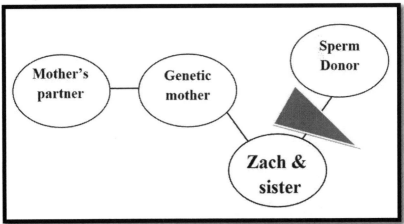

His mother and father have no relationship. The wedge between Zach and the father represents the legal system. As far as I can tell, it has permanently blocked Zach from knowing that half of his family tree. In some cases, the wedge includes falsifying the child's birth certificate with the social parent's name instead of the other genetic parent's name.

Remember this diagram? Here it is for Zach:

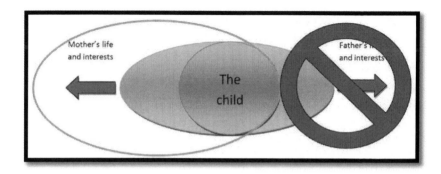

Like kids conceived by sperm donation and raised in a lesbian household, I had a social mother in addition to my genetic mother. When I was in second grade, my last name was changed to reflect my mother's new last name when she remarried. In these respects, the situation was similar between me and Zach.

On the other hand, I am not saying that our experiences are perfectly identical. For example, I did know my father and his family, I did spend time with them regularly, and his name is on my birth certificate. And Zach did not have to go back and forth between "two homes." So not identical, but similar in some important respects.

I'd like to explain one more kind of inequality that pertains only to people like Zach, those who were conceived with anonymous sperm or eggs. It is the inequality of having so many things to worry about, such as:

- Who is my donor?
- Who are my half-siblings?
- Will our paths cross?

- Will I accidentally date or marry a half-sibling?
- Where are they all?
- How many half-siblings do I have?
- Are any of them in a relationship with the donor?
- Do any of them know each other?
- Do I look like the donor and the rest of his (or her) family? Do they look like me?

It's an inequality in their family structure that their peers don't share, and that their parents never had, with stressors that their parents and their peers can hardly even imagine.

I think the main problem is that as a culture, we lost all confidence that Christianity made the right call when it came to marriage and sex. We've unhinged ourselves from the foundation that made us great and have ventured into territory that has made the idea of family dependent on adult sexual desires rather than an institution that connects children to their ontological origins. From my vantage point, it looks like the older generation took for granted the benefits they received by being raised with their own married parents, and threw all that away in order to exercise their "freedom." The kids just have to live with the consequences. Socially, long term ill effects are attributed to the kids' own lack of character. The message seems to be, "You'll get over it, just try harder. Look on the bright side: you can do the same thing to your kids."

Such "freedoms" are causing us to regress to family structures that have been repudiated because they are unjust. For example, here is what it looks like for a sperm donor with 23 children.

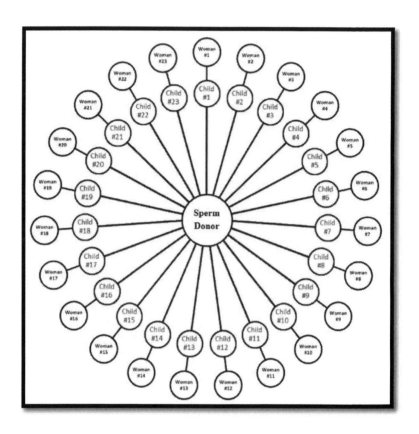

The man is the central figure, and in that way, it is similar to polygamy. Look at this diagram of the Biblical Patriarch Jacob and his family:

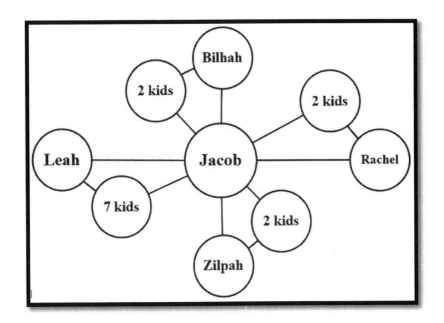

Notice how in both cases, structurally the man is the central figure. But unlike traditional polygamy, with sperm and egg donation the kids often don't know their own half-siblings or how many there are. I read one news report of somebody who believes he fathered about 800 children through sperm donation, and another report indicating that another sperm donor has fathered at least 150 children.

So, from the kids' perspective, sperm and egg donation is worse than polygamy in some important respects. The kids have less information about each other than under traditional polygamy, and are not guaranteed the protection provided by marriage between the child's father and the child's mother. Plus, there are fewer half-siblings under traditional polygamy than modern sperm/egg donation. This is not an endorsement of polygamy. I am only offering a perspective about the culture in which we find ourselves.

One of the beautiful things about the family triangle founded on natural marriage is that no one person is the central figure. Look at the next image. Contrary to what some Progressives would have you think with their cries of "The Patriarchy!" the husband/father is NOT at the center of this family structure. In fact, nobody is the central figure. But in sperm donation, the father certainly IS the central figure.

The way this is structured, all the members are equal to each other. This is true gender equality from the child's point of view.

The Sexual Revolution has blinded experts and leaders

One thing that really bothers me now is how therapeutic professionals and certain religious leaders created false expectations: they told my parents that I was "resilient," and would be "happy" if my parents were happy. I had to live under these false expectations, and when my feelings and experiences did not conform to them, I felt pathologized, as if there was something wrong with me instead of my environment.

It took me almost five decades to discover that those expectations served like a buttress, blocking me from understanding myself and the dynamic that surrounded me. I shut my mouth and towed the line as best as I could. Remember the experience I shared previously, when I was 12, standing in the driveway and had a painful realization about my life and family? I didn't share that with anybody, and it is important to understand why. There was no cultural support for me to share that kind of information. It was unwelcome. It would have revealed that I was questioning my parents' choices.

I can't help but wonder if that kind of buttress exists in the life of anybody deliberately raised outside of the intact triad. I don't blame my parents nearly as much as I blame experts and leaders who believe in sexual and reproductive liberty. My parents were just lay individuals who were honestly going about their lives. And *their* parents were divorced. They, like me, had an increased risk of experiencing their own divorces as adults, but they did not know this.

I am willing to cut my parents some slack when it comes to the structural difficulties I faced (and continue to face), but I am not willing to give slack to experts and leaders who should have known better than to give the sort of advice they were giving. They failed to take into account the negative consequences associated with sexual and reproductive liberty. Sometimes I wonder if some of these experts and leaders are more concerned about sex and being liked than they are about truth and children. I also wonder if many of them are engaging in some form of sexual liberation and so have a vested interest in maintaining it. If so, then they can't be objective about it and its harms. Any of them who claim to be Christian I hold to a much higher standard because of what I now know about the family triangle and how it corresponds to the Holy Family and the Trinity. That sort of information should be common knowledge among Christians today, yet it is not. I suspect one reason for this is the infiltration of "sexual liberation" into so many nooks and crannies of our culture. People like having no restrictions on their sexual and reproductive "choices," but since they don't bear the full cost of those "choices," they can't see the harm.

Plus, hurting my parents' feelings was *not* an option. I already had a tenuous relationship with each of them, swinging like a pendulum between them. I was not willing to jeopardize what little I felt like I had. It didn't help that I had no language or concepts to understand the situation. So even if I had the freedom, I would not have been able to express myself accurately. I was often angry and sad but didn't know why. I was supposed to be "resilient," and tried very hard to live up to that expectation.

We are so committed to the ideology of sexual, marital, and reproductive liberty that we lie to children, and kill them, to keep it afloat. As a culture, we are more worried about how adults feel about their "choices" than how the kids feel about the results of those "choices." The kids pick up on this and intuit that they can't feel something other than what the experts and adults in their lives want them to feel.

Another thing that bothers me is when people won't view these sorts of issues through anything other than the lens of social science data. They won't take a stand unless they have some social science data to support them. This means that they are willing to experiment on children.

When I think about the concepts of "sexual liberty" and "reproductive choice," I see euphemisms that uphold a "might makes right" view of children and the unborn and that undermine their rights. Those who believe in "sexual and reproductive liberty" sound like this:

"I have no obligation to be responsible with my sexual energy. If somebody is conceived due to my sexual energy, then I may or may not have an obligation to that person depending on factors I alone decide. The State has an obligation to ensure that I am free to reconstruct that person's family structure for any reason at any time, including my desire for new sex partners. I have no obligation to provide a unified home for that person. I have no obligation to maintain a relationship to that person's other genetic parent or that parent's family. If that person is still in my womb, I have the right to kill it up to the time of birth and the State has an obligation to maintain that right. Most importantly, the State has an obligation to remove all encumbrances to my sex life that I choose to have removed."

I wonder what it will take for our sexually-liberal culture to start paying attention to the disenfranchised grief of its children.

Addressing adoption and other non-triad arrangements

Even if most everybody understood what I'm saying here and agreed with it, there would still be a small amount of structural inequality among children. Death, rape, and human weakness, and ignorance means that some family structure inequality will always exist. Adoption exists to serve as a remedy for this kind of inequality.

In these discussions about why kids are not being raised with their own married mother and father, we must ask, "Why? What happened?" The answer can fall into one of two categories: "Child-centric" versus "Adult-centric." The "child-centric" category has answers like this:

- Because one or both died.
- Because one abandoned the other.
- Because one was an addict, abusive, or committing adultery.
- Because the mother was raped and wanted her baby to be raised by married parents.
- Because the child was languishing in an orphanage or foster care.

- Because the mother was young and didn't know any better.

Then we know that the custodial adults are *not* the source of the inequality. We praise those adults for taking care of those children. Adoption (and single parenting, as the case may be) in these cases is ethical. We understand that these circumstances are not the norm. They are the exception. The custodial adults also understand this. I have reason to believe that many wish that the child could have been raised with his own married mother and father, not because they view the child as a burden or are ungrateful for the child, but because they understand that the child's birthright was violated in that regard. These adults have a child-centric view of this situation.

Unfortunately, some people don't make proper distinctions at this juncture. Those child-centric circumstances are often used to justify an adult-centric practice that is not adoption and is not a legitimate form of single parenting. When this happens, it is not a way to rectify an inequality in the child's life. It is a way to give the adult something that the adult wants. For example:

- The custodial parent wanted the experience of being a parent and is willing to use money and business contracts to have that experience.
- One or both parents wanted a new sex partner.
- The custodial parent made a free and willing choice to exclude the child's other genetic parent from daily life,

even though that parent committed no grave fault that warrants such exclusion.

Instead of an attempt to rectify an inequality for the child, the custodial parents created the child or dismembered/thwarted the child's triad for their own reasons. These custodial adults don't wish that the child could have been raised with his own married mother and father.

It is also interesting to note that one category can apply to one genetic parent, while the other category applies to the other genetic parent. Rape, for example. If a woman conceived a child after being raped, I would put it in the "child-centric" category from her perspective. She should be the one who decides whether to keep and raise the child or put the child up for adoption. For the man, however, I would put it in the "adult-centric" category. Ethically he has no claim on the child, since he used his physical power to harm a woman. The child should not be raised around a man who thinks it is OK to treat women that way.

Let's look at one more difference: the screening process. In ethical adoption, the adults receive screening. Those who are unfit to be parents are screened out, or at least, that is the intention of the process. Admittedly, there are reports of the process failing at times, but at least there is a process. Failures suggest that the process needs improvement, not that it should be abandoned.

In those other practices, however, the children receive screening, not the adults. Those children who are deemed unfit to be children are aborted or thrown away as embryos. Any adult who has enough money can be a parent, including people with dangerous personality disorders and criminal histories. Furthermore, they do not have to secure the cooperation of the child's other genetic parent on a long-term basis.

"I was conceived (or raised) outside the marriage of my own mother and father. What can I do to heal?"

I am a firm believer that there are many things blocking people like us from feeling and expressing our truth. So let me tell you some of the things I've done and thought about to heal. First, I have a right to feel how I feel, but it took me a long time to feel safe enough to even think those thoughts.

Suppressing my true feelings did no good, not to me or anybody around me. In many ways, it seemed safer just to pretend that I didn't care. There is very little in the general culture that supports my true thoughts and feelings. The established narrative dictates: "You are resilient and your parents' choices about your family structure will not matter to you."

I've already mentioned one thing I discovered that was blocking me: the expectation set by professionals and experts that I would be "resilient," that I would be happy if my parents were happy, that my family structure was nothing more than a Gumby play-toy that could be molded and twisted into any shape without me caring. Believe me, I tried so hard to be what they wanted me to be, but it didn't work because that advice was based on false ideas about me.

Here are a few other blocks that I have identified: (Maybe you can think of other blocks that I have not mentioned here. I recommend writing them all down to see them clearly.)

- Fear of upsetting my family
- Lack of information about how important the triad is
- Shaming and silencing from our sexually-liberal culture
- Fear of my own anger
- Hope that my bad feelings would just go away someday
- Fear of appearing disloyal to my parents
- Not wanting to feel like a victim
- Being afraid to imagine my parents together

Once I identified my blocks, I decided to try and dislodge them. One way for me to do that was to put my mom and dad together in my mind and in my heart. They are the origin of who I am, after all. I am not a disembodied spirit, with a soul that could have been incarnated into a different body. My soul and my body are intimately linked. Since my body is not divided, then the origins of my body can't be divided without doing damage to my self-image. And that is precisely what happened when they split up. It was as if something inside me became ruptured. Even after decades have gone by, I still feel it. Yet, when I imagine them together, it helps a little, like a salve. I know it's not real in one sense, yet somehow it is real, since I am real.

The "one-flesh" unity of my mom and my dad was supposed to be like a mirror for me, to see myself fully and in a holistic way. Imagine if my left hand worried about what my right foot was doing. That sounds ridiculous, right? But it is a good analogy for what it was like for me to live in a situation where my genetic parents had rejected each other. That triad was an organic whole. Shattering it shattered a "mirror" I desperately needed so that I could see myself and orient myself within my family.

As a way to show respect to children, we are supposed to be part of the one-flesh unity of our own mother and father. Our culture of sex, along with many experts and leaders, tells mothers and fathers that they do not need to show their children that sort of respect. So when mothers and fathers fail in that duty, it is not all their fault. Cultures exert powerful influences, and even governments are involved in destroying that triad, failing to defend it, and giving incentives for it to not form. There is a lot working against the family.

Writing this report was therapeutic. Putting all my thoughts and observations to paper in a coherent form has helped me see that I am not crazy and I am not alone. Plus, I have used my life story to make an argument for something I believe in. I feel good knowing I might help others make better decisions about themselves and their children.

Since I have rejected sexual liberty and the culture of sex it fuels, I am free to reject its taboo surrounding discussions about its bad results. My voice has gotten stronger because it reflects more of who I am. When I was younger and less educated about these issues, my voice was diminished. This is because I was inadvertently accepting the negative consequences without fully examining them and seeing how much they were influencing me. For example, the culture of sex required me to cut off half of myself for the sake of others, so they could be "free," and would never feel uncomfortable about the choices they made.

Imagine dipping a baby into a tub of Clorox and letting him sit there for a while. The baby cries because his skin gets burned, but we don't say he's crazy for crying. Unfortunately, this is roughly what it was like for me. I was put into a painful and impossible situation, I reacted to it negatively, then was faulted for having negative reactions. Again, it's not entirely my parents' fault. Experts and leaders assured them what they were doing was OK.

Given everything I've said here, ask yourself a couple questions: What sort of contribution do you want to make? What do you think is most fair to *all* generations, not just the one in power?

"I've created an inequality for my child. Now what?"

You are not alone. I am divorced, and so I created an inequality for my own children. I understand the dilemma. Let me borrow from the pro-life movement again. Some post-abortive women regret their abortions. Some doctors who performed abortions stopped doing them because they realized what they were doing. And some of those people want to speak out about it, to tell the truth about what happened and what they did, to become advocates for positive change.

I see myself sort of like that. I am divorced. Think of me as the equivalent of the post-abortive woman, but for divorce and other forms of fractured families. I hope it is obvious how much I can relate to other "alternative" family forms! There is nothing wrong with speaking about structural problems you faced and repenting from harms you did, then becoming an advocate for change. People do it all the time. There *is* a way forward for you. I feel very confident about that. I will tell you how it worked for me.

First, I repented of my sins. This is the most important step. I became a Catholic in 2012, and we have a robust view of sin and repentance, what each of those things are, and what one needs to do to be forgiven. I sincerely followed what my Church teaches on those matters. One of the great things about repentance is that I saw things more and more clearly. The more I dug down into my sins and sincerely repented of them, the more clearly I could see all of what I am telling you here, and more. Before I repented, it was as if I had been driving a car with a muddied windshield. Repentance was like the water that washed the mud away. I could see so clearly! It was amazing.

Next, when I reflect on how my own children do not experience the family structure that reflects the Holy Family and the Trinity, I go to God and tell Him that it hurts. I can honestly say that I have repented from my own activities that damaged the relationship with their father, and I pray for my children every single day. I also pray for their father and his family. I ask my kids about them, and let them know that he is welcome in my home if he ever wants to come here to talk, or also on holidays and birthdays. I am also friends with a few of his family members on Facebook. He and I have apologized to each other, and I wrote him a letter a few months ago, expressing again my regret at my mistakes and asking for his friendship for the sake of our children (and now, a grandchild). I don't want my kids to feel like I have rejected one-half of who they are, one-half of their lives, and to the extent that I have, I want to minimize it as much as possible. There are many details about my ex-husband and the marriage that I have not shared here, since doing so would detract from my point about *my* need for repentance. Regardless of my ex-husband, I still had serious sins from which I needed to repent.

One of the things I've found difficult about being a parent is the realization of how much I've hurt my own children. That kind of pain doesn't go away.

Next, when I feel the pain of having a permanently disfigured genetic family, I pray for my parents and ask for healing for myself. I go to confession and confess my anger about it. I know that someday God will remove it, or show me what else I need to do so that He can remove it.

I carry these crosses as well as I can. Mostly I think I carry them with a good attitude, but sometimes not. I might be happy one day, then fall into sadness or self-pity another day. I always try to give the suffering to God. It becomes a penance. One of the great things about the Catholic faith is that the Church has taught me what to do with pain and sorrow. It doesn't have to be wasted.

I have total confidence that God sees everything that happened, and this gives me great comfort. Nothing escapes His gaze, and everything will be accounted for eventually, sort of like the way a good accountant keeps track of everything on the balance sheet with great care and attention to detail. I trust in His timing! He has shown me over and over that He sees it all and He has not forgotten any of my tears and prayers. I now understand that some important things will not be fixed in this life, and that is OK.

Joy and peace are still part of my daily walk, especially when I put my trust in Him.

Next, I try to let my children have their own experiences, and I try to be careful that I am not insisting that their feelings about the breakup of their genetic family conform to my expectations. There is no question that the divorce hurt them deeply, and that the disfigurement of their family is a permanently painful condition that will affect them for the rest of their lives. I try to be very careful and accommodating around the holidays and birthdays, remembering how hard it is for me to navigate those times, even still.

Even so, one person cannot create this sort of equality on his or her own. It requires two people, the mother and the father, willingly working together. If one of them does not want to participate in creating this kind of equality after a child has been born, then there is little the other can do. Remaining positive and keeping a door open for friendship can't hurt in most cases.

Diagrams of structural inequalities in well-known families

Here are a few other diagrams that are based on the family triangle. First is President Donald Trump's family. I predict that we will see less of Tiffany Trump than we do the other children during his presidency. She is the most weakly linked of all of them.

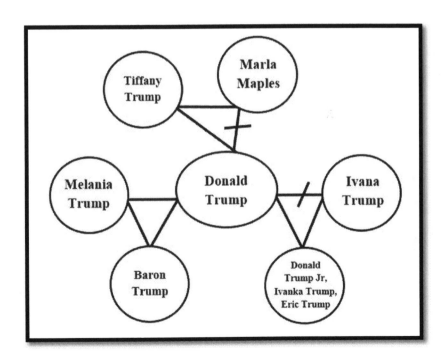

Here is the actor Donald Sutherland and his family. The first marriage (not shown) had no children and that wife died a year after they divorced. Kiefer Sutherland, a famous actor in his own right, was part of Donald's second marriage to Shirley Douglas. Francine Racette is his third wife.

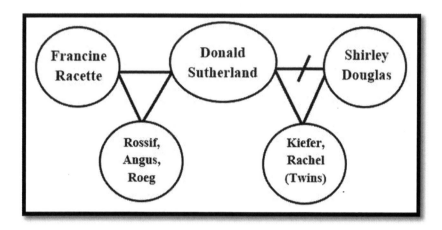

Here we see former President Barack Obama's family.

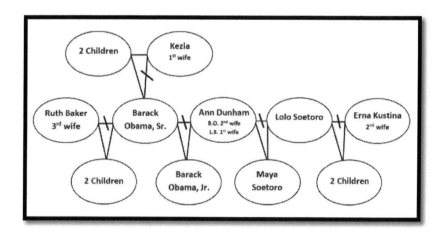

Actress Lindsay Lohan and her family.

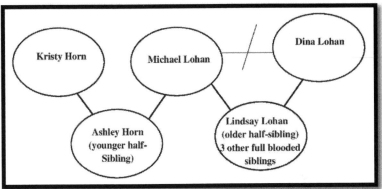

From the Bible, Abraham and his family.

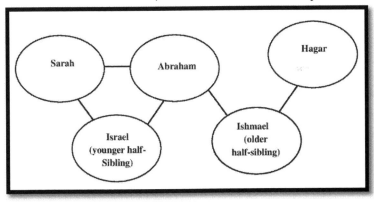

Elton John and his family.

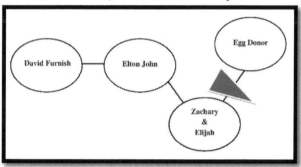

Next we have somebody from the business world named Kenneth Lay. He was the CEO for Enron, and was implicated in a well-known accounting scandal that came to light in the early 2000s. There is a book about this scandal, called, *The Smartest Guys in the Room*. Lay, who was married to Judie and had two children with her, had an affair with his divorced secretary Linda in about 1980. He filed for divorce from Judie in order to marry Linda. Judie spent the early phases of the divorce proceedings in hospitals as a result of a manic-depressive illness caused by the impending divorce. The divorce "hit her very hard" and she said "it was like dying." She later recovered and said that Ken treated her "very nicely." In 2006, Lay was convicted of crimes as a result of the accounting scandal, but died of a heart attack before sentencing.

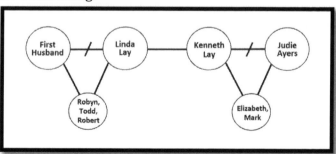

Next are three fictional families. The first is Cinderella's family. I don't know if Cinderella's step mother was considered a widow or a divorcée. Her father was depicted as a widower.

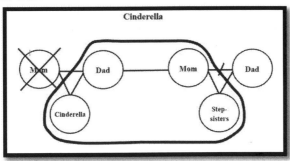

Next is the Brady family. The story goes that the original Mrs. Brady died. But Mr. Martin, who was Carol Brady's first husband, is never quite accounted for. The creator of the show, Sherwood Schwartz, wanted Mrs. Brady depicted as a divorcée, but being remarried as a divorcée was considered a scandal at that time. Her status was never addressed during the show one way or the other. In either case, the girls took their stepdad's last name, which was an injustice to them in my opinion, thereby setting a bad example for the general culture. If this had happened in real life, it is doubtful that Mr. Martin or his family would have appreciated having the girls' last name changed.

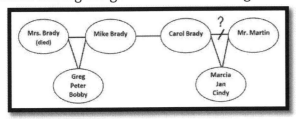

The next diagram depicts a fictional character named Troy Phelan and his family, from John Grisham's novel, *The Testament*. The diagram does not include the babies that were aborted due to Troy's affairs with unnamed mistresses.

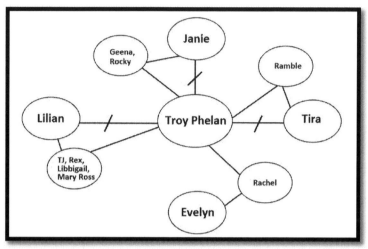

Finally, here is a hypothetical step-family arrangement. Notice that two formerly intact families now comprise three households.

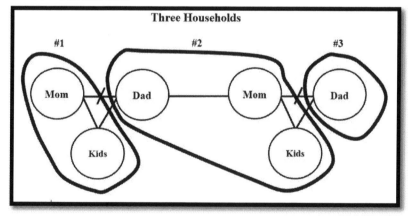

Tips for creating your own
family structure diagrams

At first, have several pieces of blank paper on hand. Depending on the complexity of your situation, it may take more than one attempt to create the diagram accurately.

This model works best with two generations, not three or more. Plan accordingly.

Here is how to represent siblings:

- Exclude the older generation's full-blooded siblings from the diagram. If desired, create a different diagram with one of those siblings in either the first or second generation.

- For the younger generation, always put full-blooded siblings inside the same circle. The point of this exercise is to examine the structure of the family. Placing full-blooded siblings in their own circles potentially introduces interpersonal family dynamics into the argument. One of the objectives of this exercise is to exclude interpersonal family dynamics so that family structure can be examined in a pure way.

- Half-siblings will always share one parent, and will have another genetic parent who is not shared between them. This is why half-siblings each have their own circle.

- Putting full-blooded siblings inside the same circle, and putting half-blooded siblings in separate circles, makes it clear how different the structure of the family is for each of them.

- Step-siblings will not share either genetic parent.

Represent divorce by first showing the marriage as a line between the spouses. Then draw a perpendicular (or nearly perpendicular) line through the marriage line. If the genetic parents were never married, don't connect them with a line.

There are a couple different ways to start. One way is to consider the person who has had the most sex partners that resulted in children who are half-siblings to each other. Draw the family structure around that person. Another way to start is with the person who has had to deal with the most complexity in their family structure. Draw the family structure around that person. See the above diagrams of President Donald Trump and President Barack Obama for examples of what I mean.

We can do better for minor children

There is a lot of family structure inequality among minor children, and it is only getting worse as "sexual and reproductive liberty" continues unabated. There can never be 100% structural equality among minor children because of death, human weakness, ignorance, and in rare cases, necessity. Even so, we can do a lot better than we are doing now. Improving family structure equality among minor children won't be easy, but an important step will include the widespread rejection of "sexual and reproductive liberty." Like a factory that makes more profit when it doesn't have to account for the pollution it causes, adults who exercise "sexual and reproductive liberty" receive the benefits while pushing the negative consequences onto subsequent generations.

Questions and objections

"Conservatives are not attracted to equality-based arguments, and liberals are not attracted to the defense of natural marriage. Isn't this going to be a problem for the advancement of this argument?"

Possibly. On its surface, the argument probably does not immediately appeal to either camp, but I hope it can build a bridge between them. Conservatives can use this argument to help liberals understand what natural marriage provides to children, and liberals can use this argument to help conservatives appreciate the value of equality. Since it is a bridge between the two camps, each gets something in exchange for a concession. Conservatives concede that equality is an important ideal, and liberals concede that natural marriage matters. In exchange, conservatives gain more adherents to the value of natural marriage, and liberals gain more adherents to the value of equality.

"What about the times where a person has minor children from a previous marriage (or other relationship), and that person is free to marry? Are you saying they cannot marry? They would be creating an inequality, after all."

I am a Catholic, so let me plainly state that I do not intend to present something here that is contrary to what the Catholic Church teaches.

If a parent of minor children is free to marry, then I am not forbidding marriage. For one thing, I do not have authority to forbid marriage, nor do I desire such authority. I am only offering information so that the parent can make an informed decision as to the best course of action *for all parties involved*. This, of course, includes minor children from prior marriages or other relationships. Too often, parents accept false ideas about children's resiliency and what is owed to children, and they are not properly trained to understand what a new marriage actually creates for a child in terms of family structure. Just because the parent has "moved on" from a prior relationship does not mean that the child has, or that the child must. Given our sexually lax culture, parents of minor children take too much for granted in this respect, in my opinion. I only seek to rectify this deficiency so that single parents of minor children who are free to marry may make more informed long-term decisions.

"Are you saying that people in a second sacramental marriage, when there are minor children from a prior marriage or other relationship, are sinning or have done something wrong?"

This is a complex question and I have a lot to say about it. The short answer is that, given the parameters as stated in the question, the marriage is not a sin. However, I am shining a light into an area where little light has shone. I don't expect parents of minor children in current second marriages, even sacramental marriages, to already be acquainted with the argument I present here.

Part of the problem is that, in my opinion, family courts may not be creating separation and custody agreements that are in accordance with divine law. "No fault" divorce means that a petitioning spouse is the judge in his own case regarding cessation of conjugal living and the need for permanent separation. "No fault" means that family courts enforce the petitioner's private judgement regarding those matters. The respondent in a "no fault" divorce action has no legal means to defend against the action. Isn't this contrary to the public nature of marriage? Thus, I do not fault parents who are entering into new marriages with minor children—who are creating the sort of inequality I argue against here—in ignorance and good faith. I firmly believe that:

- parents have not been given the full understanding of what sort of family structure they are creating for their minor child when they marry somebody who is not the child's other genetic parent.
- the family court system in the United States is not providing justice to divorcing parents, which then creates more problems.
- leaders and professionals have not spoken against divorce and remarriage nearly enough.
- the general population believes false ideas about children and what is owed to them (for example, "Kids are resilient," "Babies are blank slates").
- The average person in this situation does not understand that divorce is harder for children to cope with than the death of one parent. I believe that this is because divorce splits the child's family tree into two distinct parts that reject each other. Death does not do this.

Taken together, this is a recipe for the kind of inequality I argue against. Here are four thought experiments parents can do to evaluate the level of equality being given to children under their care who have different parents:

1. Look at the family photos on the wall and see whose full families are represented there and whose are not.
2. Think about which children live in a unified home with both genetic parents, and which live in "two homes," meaning that from the child's perspective, he or she does not have one parent who is a daily 24/7, full-time parent.
3. Compare the names of the parents on the children's birth certificates.
4. Consider how inheritances will flow to the children if a spouse, grandparent, or other relative from an older generation died today.

These thought experiments may reveal which children are being treated as full-fledged family members in that family, and which are not. Being kind to a child is not the same thing as treating a child as a full-fledged family member.

"It sounds like you expect single parents to remain single for their whole lives."

If they are free to marry, I do not expect them to remain single for their whole lives, and I am unable and incompetent to forbid something that St. Paul and the Church permits. Whatever exceptions St. Paul and the Church permit are meant to be precisely that: exceptions that are permitted because of a prior tragedy or failure, not the normative way families should be formed. It is also important to understand that if something is permitted, this does not mean it is required. While I do not intend to place an unnecessary burden on parents, I firmly believe that our hyper-sexualized culture encourages parents to place burdens on their minor children, by marrying at a time that does not work for the child, and marrying somebody who is not a suitable stepparent. On the other hand, I hope nobody ever uses this argument to hurt a parent who is free to marry. I see how that could happen.

Even if my parents had been free to marry after they divorced each other, everything else being the same, this would not have changed the subsequent chaos for me, nor would it have provided me with one full time, 24/7 parent. Thus, I only ask that single parents of minor children who are free to marry prayerfully consider the timing for dating, courtship, and marriage. For example, might it be best to refrain from dating, courtship, and marriage until the children are fully launched into their adult lives? Might it be best for the children if the parents focus on ensuring that they are fully prepared for their adult lives and careers by completing their educations (such as obtaining post-high school degrees or obtaining vocational certifications), or have gotten married? For parents of minor children who are free to marry, it is a question of timing, not ability. Speaking for myself, I was deeply offended that each of my parents spent more time with their new love interests than they did with me. I hope that all parents of minor children, whose other genetic parent lives, will see the difficulty that new relationships impose on children.

On a related note, I would also request that once the parent marries, and regardless of the age of the child, they consider ensuring that any inheritances that would have flowed to the children if their families had remained intact, continue to flow to the children. This may require special legal arrangements, since the new spouse may have a legal claim on these pre-marriage assets. I have heard stories of parents assuming that the stepparents would take care of everything appropriately, but did not. The children have already suffered the injustice of a dismembered family and all of the obfuscation that accompanied it. I don't think it is fair to saddle them with the injustice of losing their inheritance, as long as it is reasonable to predict that they would have received an inheritance had the first family remained intact.

"This argument can apply to other configurations besides the triangle, such as some other form of polygon."

I can only address this objection in a general way, since no specific polygon was proposed. I hope it is clear by now that I am making an argument based on respecting a child's ontology. The one-flesh union of a child's mother and father serves this purpose. It is like a mirror for the child to see and orient himself as he grows. Thus, in terms of having one's ontology respected; of having the parental one-flesh union being an accurate reflection of one's ontology (like a mirror); of being connected to one's origins, culture, and language; of knowing who one resembles; of having a truly unified home without extraneous parental figures to attend to outside of that home; and of having an intact genetic family tree, the triangle provides the most justice for children. Any other polygon will provide less justice in those respects. Yes, in principle, we *could* make an argument for equality of some other configuration, but with respect to the issues I mentioned, there is no other configuration that equals the triangle, and all others provide less justice in varying degrees.

"What is the difference between the sacrament of marriage and natural marriage? Why do you only defend natural marriage and not the sacrament of marriage?"

Let me use an analogy. Imagine a one-layer cake, and frosting on that layer. The cake layer is natural marriage and the frosting is the sacrament. Marriage between two non-baptized people, or one baptized and one non-baptized, is like the cake layer without the frosting. Marriage between two who are baptized is like the cake layer with the frosting. The sacrament sort of "rests" on top of natural marriage, like the frosting rests on top of the cake layer. The sacrament of marriage, the frosting, doesn't exist without that first layer—if there is no marriage then there is no sacrament. By making my defense explicitly about natural marriage, I automatically defend the sacrament of marriage without needing to mention it.

"Full-blooded siblings have different experiences in their own families. You shouldn't put them all in one circle in the diagram. They should have their own circles."

I appreciate the objection, because it allows me to explain why I have excluded interpersonal family interactions from the argument. I've noticed that people often conflate interpersonal family dynamics with family structure. By creating the diagrams the way I have, I can examine what different family structures provide (or fail to provide) to children in terms of their ontology, apart from the parent's character or behavior within that family.

While it is true that full-blooded siblings have their own experiences, they do not have different family structures. Putting full-blooded siblings together in one circle makes it clear that they all have the same exact *structure* of their family—there is family structure equality between them. In families where there are also half and/or step-siblings, creating individual circles for each full-blooded sibling:

- Might communicate a level of family structure equality between all of the siblings that does not exist.
- Is not necessary, since the argument excludes interpersonal family dynamics.
- Might make the argument less clear; potentially introduces interpersonal family dynamics into it.

Try drawing it, using one of the examples presented here, and see if you agree.

"I tried to create a diagram with my children, me, and my parents, but it didn't work very well."

This model works best when used with only two generations. For example, draw one with you and your parents, or your children and you. All the diagrams presented here are two-generation diagrams.

"In regards to the diagrams here, are you making an assertion regarding which marriages are valid versus which are invalid from a Catholic perspective?"

No.

Interesting quotes

"It took me a long time to realize the following truth: No matter how compassionate, charitable, winsome, and kind you are, if you oppose the sexual revolution you are the enemy." David French (2012)

"...when religious liberty and sexual liberty conflict, [Feldblum] admits, 'I'm having a hard time coming up with any case in which religious liberty should win.' ... 'Sexual liberty should win in most cases. There can be a conflict between religious liberty and sexual liberty, but in almost all cases the sexual liberty should win because that's the only way that the dignity of gay people can be affirmed in any realistic manner.'" Chai Feldblum in an interview with Maggie Gallagher (2006)

"In extremely invalidating environments, parents or caregivers do not teach children to discriminate effectively between what they feel and what the caregivers feel, what the child wants and what the caregiver wants (or wants the child to want), what the child thinks and what the caregiver thinks." Fruzzetti, Shenk & Hoffman (2005)

"I say nothing of father, for he is shrouded in a mystery I have never been able to penetrate. Slavery does away with fathers as it does away with families... The order of civilization is reversed here. The name of the child is not expected to be that of its father... He can be father without being a husband and may sell his child without incurring reproach..." Frederick Douglass, *My Bondage and My Freedom* (1855)

"The Servile State... has always been embarrassed by the institution of marriage. It is an old story that the negro slavery of 'Uncle Tom's Cabin' did its worst work in the breaking-up of families. But curiously enough, the same story is told from both sides. For the apologists of the Slave States, or, at least, of the Southern States, make the same admission even in their own defence (sic). If they denied breaking up the slave family, it was because they denied there was any slave family to break up. Free love is the direct enemy of freedom. It is the most obvious of all the bribes that can be offered by slavery. In servile societies, a vast amount of sexual laxity can go on in practice... One of the conveniences of that pagan world is that, below a certain level of society, nobody really need bother about pedigree or paternity at all... of all the bribes that the old pagan slavery can offer, this luxury and laxity is the strongest..." G.K. Chesterton, *Fancies versus Fads* (1923)

"...sexual liberty does seem to lead to sexual injustice... As much as I love sexual liberty and wouldn't want any less of it, I think it has to be acknowledged that certain forms of social sexual constraints block some of these [undesired] effects. When sex takes place only in monogamous marriages (gay or straight), there's a huge levelling off... If everyone has to pair off, this removes the more attractive people from the pool of partners. So if you're one of the people less likely to be found attractive, there will be others around of your preferred sex/gender who might want to pair off with you." Patricia Marino (2015)

"One of the fallouts of feminism is that girls became more accessible. Maybe not wisely accessible. A lot of young girls—they're expected to give blow jobs now. Young, young girls, as far as I can perceive. Maybe 12 or 13 years old. I mean, that's a rite of passage, I suppose. As a feminist, I don't want those girls to be used. Maybe they love giving blow jobs, I don't know. Maybe they do? But I don't think you really love giving boys in general blow jobs without any feeling to someone you're not close to. I don't try to speak for people that young. I'm not that young anymore. But my own sense of self—I wouldn't give myself away that easily. That's part of the culture, and I don't like that it's put on teenyboppers and young girls." Lily Tomlin (2013)

"With the greatly increased 'sexual freedom' there is more post-coital depression and greater inability to relate in non-genital ways. These sexually, or rather genitally, hyperactive persons are more lonely and isolated from each other. They frustrate each other in their promiscuous pursuit of the goal: to feel loved and wanted. The 'joys of sex' are accompanied by intensified feelings of fear, worry, anxiety, tension, hate, loneliness, depression and despair." Conrad Baars, M.D., *Feeling and Healing Your Emotions* (1979)

"Hookup culture [on college campuses] is an occupying force, coercive and omnipresent. For those who live it, it's all sunshine, but it isn't for everyone else. Deep in the fog, students often feel dreary, confused, helpless. Many behave in ways they don't like, hurt people unwillingly, and consent to sexual activity they don't desire... In response [to the hookup culture], many students opt out of hooking up, but they can't opt out of hookup culture. It's more than just a behavior; it's the climate. It can't be wished away any more than we can wish away a foggy day." Lisa Wade, *American Hookup: The New Culture of Sex on Campus* (2017)

"The whole of human history does not contain a single instance of a group becoming civilized unless it has been absolutely monogamous, nor is there any example of a group retaining its culture after it has adopted less rigorous customs." J.D. Unwin, *Monogamy as a Condition of Social Energy* (1927)

"Any human society is free to choose either to display great energy or to enjoy sexual freedom; the evidence is that it cannot do both for more than one generation." J. D. Unwin, *Sex and Culture* (1934)

"'...Respecting a child's dignity means affirming his or her need and natural right to have a mother and a father.' We are speaking not simply of the love of father and mother as individuals, but also of their mutual love, perceived as the source of one's life and the solid foundation of the family." Amoris Laetitia 172

A gift for you

You've made it this far, so I have a gift for you. It is a PDF download called, "You Were Loved into Existence."

No matter what our family circumstances are, God has loved us *all* into existence! That's another form of equality, another way we are all the same. You can receive this free PDF download by signing up for the Ruth Institute's e-newsletter here:

www.RuthNewsletter.org

Unsubscribe at any time. Please accept this PDF as a gift from all of us at the Ruth Institute.

Bibliography

Allen, D. M. (2013, September 23). *Invalidation in Families: What Are The Hidden Aspects?* Retrieved from Psychology Today: https://www.psychologytoday.com/blog/matter-personality/201309/invalidation-in-families-what-are-the-hidden-aspects

Anonymous. (2015, December 22). *Going Home For The Holidays Is Tough When Your Family Is Broken.* Retrieved from I Believe In Love: http://www.ibelieveinlove.com/2015/12/22/going-home-for-the-holidays-is-tough-when-your-family-is-broken/

Attachment Theory. (n.d.). Retrieved from University of East Anglia: Secure Base.

Barber, J., & Hertz, F. (2016). *Will my stepmother's children claim my father's estate?* Retrieved from Caring.com: https://www.caring.com/questions/stepmothers-children-inherit-fathers-estate

Brennan, S. (2017, July 24). Would YOU pay your stepchild's private school fees? *Daily Mail.*

Burkett, B. (2014, August 19). *On Civilizations and Sex.* Retrieved from Ethika Politika: https://ethikapolitika.org/2014/08/19/civilizations-sex/

Childress, C. (2014, August 19). Parental Alienation: An Attachment-based Model. Irvine, California: California Southern

University. Retrieved from
https://www.youtube.com/watch?v=brNuwQNN3q4

Fagan, P., & Churchill, A. (2012). *The Effects of Divorce on Children.*
Marriage and Religion Research Institute.

Farrow, D. (2007). *Nation of Bastards: Essays on the End of
Marriage.* Toronto: BPS Books.

Faulkner, J. (2013). *Making Sure: Sterilzation for the Severely Fertile.*
Retrieved from Fit Pregnancy and Baby:
https://www.fitpregnancy.com/pregnancy/labor-
delivery/ask-labor-nurse/making-sure

Fetters, A. (2017, January 16). *Thanks, Obama, for 4 Years of
Glorious, Worry-Free Sex.* Retrieved from GQ.com:
http://www.gq.com/story/thanks-obama-sex

Flesburg, E. O. (2008). *The Switching Hour: Kids of Divorce Say
Goodbye Again.* Nashville: Abingdon Press.

Fontana, M. (2015, September 16). *Surprise Speech with Ryan T.
Anderson: The Cost of Equality*. Retrieved from YouTube:
https://www.youtube.com/watch?v=wGPlHdzHPFE

Garcia, C. (2011). *When Tubal Ligations and Vascectomies Fail.*
Retrieved from Babble:
https://www.babble.com/pregnancy/tubal-ligation-tubes-
tied-vasectomy-sterilization-surgery-fail/

Gergis, S., Anderson, R. T., & George, R. P. (2012). *What is
Marriage? Man and Woman: A Defense.* New York:
Encounter Books.

Haidt, J. (2012). *The Righteous Mind: Why Good People are Divided by Politics and Religion.* New York: Vintage Books.

James, S. D. (2011, February 3). *Son of Iowa Lesbians Fights Gay Marriage Ban.* Retrieved from ABC News: http://abcnews.go.com/Health/zach-wahls-son-lesbians-speech-anti-gay-legislators/story?id=12832200

Johnson, J. (2015). *Reflections on Christian Equality.* Retrieved from The Christian Post: http://www.christianpost.com/news/reflections-on-christian-equality-140644/

Kanazawa, S. (2011, January 9). *Why Are Stepparents More Likely to Kill Their Children?* Retrieved from Psychology Today: https://www.psychologytoday.com/blog/the-scientific-fundamentalist/201101/why-are-stepparents-more-likely-kill-their-children

Kelly, J. (2016, September 23). Kids First: How to Put Children Ahead of Broken Relationships. *UVA Today.*

Lopez, R. O. (2015). *Jephthah's Daughters: Innocent Casualties in the War for Family 'Equality'.* Northridge: CreateSpace.

Marquardt, E. (2006). *Between Two Worlds: The Inner Lives of Children of Divorce.* New York: Three Rivers Press.

Marquardt, E., Glenn, N., & Clark, K. (2010). *My Daddy's Name is Donor: A New Study of Young Adults Conceived Through Sperm Donation.* New York: Institute for American Values.

McKenzie, R. B. (2014). *Foster Care versus Modern Orphanages.* Washington, D.C.: National Center for Policy Analysis.

Meldrum-Hanna, C. (2013, February 7). *Disturbing child abuse case links Australians to paedophile ring.* Retrieved from Australian Broadcasting Commission: http://www.abc.net.au/7.30/content/2013/s3794616.htm

Miller, J. (2013, March 18). *Lily Tomlin on Why 'Girls' is Too Sexual.* Retrieved from Vanity Fair: http://www.vanityfair.com/hollywood/2013/03/lily-tomlin-admission-tina-fey-lena-dunham-girls

Miller, L. (2017). *Primal Loss: The Now-Adult Children of Divorce Speak.* Phoenix: LCB Publishing.

Morse, J. R. (2009). *Love and Economics: It Takes a Family to Raise a Village.* San Marcos: Ruth Institute Books.

Morton, N., & Bell, S. (2016, January 13). I fathered 800 children, claims sperm donor. *BBC News.*

Mroz, J. (2011, September 5). One Sperm Donor, 150 Offspring. *New York Times.*

Newman, A. (2017). *Stories.* Retrieved from Anonymous Us: https://anonymousus.org/stories/

Pope Paul IV, S. J. (1987). *Humanae Vitae: A Challenge to Love.* Detroit: New Hope.

Roam, D. (2010). *Bla Bla Bla: What To Do When Words Don't Work.* London: Penguin Books.

Root, A. (2010). *The Children of Divorce: Loss of Family As The Loss Of Being.* Grand Rapids: Baker Academic.

Schlessinger, L. (2014, August 21). *11 Rules for Dating After Divorce.* Retrieved from DrLaura.com:

https://www.drlaura.com/b/11-Rules-for-Dating-After-a-Divorce/-247679268819415333.html

Sherman, M. (2014, June 20). *Why We Don't Give Each Other a Break*. Retrieved from Psychology Today: https://www.psychologytoday.com/blog/real-men-dont-write-blogs/201406/why-we-dont-give-each-other-break

Solomon, J., & George, C. (1999). The development of attachment in separated and divorce families. Effects of overnight visitation, parent and couple variables. *PubMed*.

Sorge, J. (Director). (2014). *Divorce Corp* [Motion Picture].

Ssshhh - Don't mention family structure. (2017, January 19). Retrieved from New Zealand Herald: http://m.nzherald.co.nz/northland-age/news/article.cfm?c_id=1503402&objectid=11785092

Stern, M. J. (2017, February 16). *Federal Judge Orders South Carolina to List Same-Sex Parents on Birth Certificates*. Retrieved from Slate: http://www.slate.com/blogs/outward/2017/02/16/federal_judge_orders_south_carolina_to_list_same_sex_parents_on_birth_certificates.html

Stowe, H. B. (1995). *Uncle Tom's Cabin*. London: Wordsworth.

Tuttle, I. (2014, June 24). *State Dept LGBT Speaker: We Don't Want Gay Marriage; We Want No Marriage*. Retrieved from National Review: http://www.nationalreview.com/corner/381148/state-dept-lgbt-speaker-we-dont-want-gay-marriage-we-want-no-marriage-ian-tuttle van Gennep, A. (1960). *The Rites of Passage.* Chicago: University of Chicago Press.

Wahls, Z. (2012). *My Two Moms: Lessons of Love, Strength, and What Makes a Family.* New York: Gotham Books.

Wallerstein, J. (2001). *The Unexpected Legacy of Divorce: The 25 Year Landmark Study.* New York: Hyperion.

Warshak, R. A. (2010). *Divorce Poison New and Updated Version: How to Protect Your Family from Bad-mouthing and Brainwashing.* New York: Harper Collins.

Yancy, P. (1994, December 2). *The Lost Sex Study.* Retrieved from Christianity Today: http://www.christianitytoday.com/ct/1994/december12/4te080.html

About the author, Jennifer Johnson

Jennifer Johnson's life story fits well with the mission of the Ruth Institute, which is to create a Christ-like mass social movement to end the agony and injustice of family breakdown.

As a young adult, she dropped out of UC Santa Barbara to join a small fundamentalist Bible-church that gradually morphed into a Gnostic personality cult. This group appealed to her deep longing for stability and belonging. For the first time, she felt like a full-fledged member of a "family." Even though the spiritual and emotional price to be there was steep, she was willing to pay it for that sense of belonging and to avoid confronting the chaos of her childhood. While there, she had an arranged marriage, had three children, and homeschooled them for nine years. She had a few homeschooling articles published in *Practical Homeschooling* in the mid 2000s. She was thrown out of the cult in 2008, and her husband did not follow her out. She filed for divorce a few months later.

The same month that she filed for divorce, she consciously refrained from voting Yes on California's Proposition 8, the initiative to define marriage as between one man and one woman. During this time, she wrote and self-published several e-books about *QuickBooks Financial Software,* while slowly building up her small bookkeeping practice. In 2010, she sold that practice and accepted a full-time position with the Ruth Institute as its Director of Operations. This initiated an unexpected spiritual mentorship with its founder, Jennifer Roback Morse, Ph.D. Dr. Morse's influence was instrumental in bringing her into full communion with the Catholic Church in 2012. She has served as the Treasurer for the Ruth Institute since 2013. In 2016, she graduated from Edison State University with a B.S.B.A.

53001207R00059

Made in the USA
Lexington, KY
23 September 2019